Robot
Universe

By Lynn Huggins-Cooper

US Senior Editor Shannon Beatty
Senior Editor Sam Priddy
Editors Kritika Gupta, Kathleen Teece
Project Art Editor Yamini Panwar
Art Editors Emma Hobson, Roohi Rais, Shubham Rohatgi
Jacket Coordinator Francesca Young
Jacket Designers Dheeraj Arora, Amy Keast
DTP Designers Vijay Kandwal, Dheeraj Singh
Picture Researcher Aditya Katyal
Producer, Pre-Production Marina Hartung
Producer Niamh Tierney
Managing Editors Monica Saigal, Laura Gilbert
Managing Art Editors Neha Ahuja Chowdhry, Diane Peyton Jones
Art Director Martin Wilson
Publisher Sarah Larter
Publishing Director Sophie Mitchell

Robotics Consultant Helmut Hauser
Reading Consultant Linda Gambrell

First American Edition, 2017
Published in the United States by DK Publishing
345 Hudson Street, New York, New York 10014
Copyright © 2017 Dorling Kindersley Limited
DK, a Penguin Random House Company
17 18 19 20 21 10 9 8 7 6 5 4 3 2 1
001–299006–Nov/17

A catalog record for this book is available from the Library of Congress.
ISBN: 978-1-4654-6321-0 (Paperback)
ISBN: 978-1-4654-6320-3 (Hardcover)

DK books are available at special discounts when purchased in bulk for sales promotions,
premiums, fund-raising, or educational use. For details, contact:
DK Publishing Special Markets,
345 Hudson Street, New York, New York 10014
SpecialSales@dk.com

Printed and bound in China.

The publisher would like to thank the following for their kind permission to reproduce their photographs:
(Key: a-above; b-below/bottom; c-center; f-far; l-left; r-right; t-top)

1 From/by Softbank Robotics. **3** Dorling Kindersley: Geoff Brightling / Department of Electrical and Electronic Engineering, University of Portsmouth (br). **5** Rex
Shutterstock: Tom Nicholson (b). **7** Alamy Stock Photo: Polly Thomas (b). **8** 123RF.com: Viktoriya Sukhanova (cb). Dorling Kindersley: Department of Cybernetics, University
of Reading (c, b). **8-9** 123RF.com: Viktoriya Sukhanova (c). **9** 123RF.com: Viktoriya Sukhanova (bc). Dorling Kindersley: Department of Cybernetics, University of Reading
(cra). **10** Alamy Stock Photo: North Wind Picture Archives (br). **11** Alamy Stock Photo: KUCO (br). **12** Getty Images: Universal History Archive (bl). **13** Getty Images: DEA
DAGLI ORTI (ca). **15** Rex Shutterstock: Everett Kennedy Brown / EPA (r). **16** Alamy Stock Photo: ART Collection (br); Science History Images (cl). **17** 123RF.com: Georgi
Kollidas (tl). Alamy Stock Photo: ART Collection (cr); Pictorial Press Ltd (bc). **18** Getty Images: Science & Society Picture Library (bl). **19** Getty Images: Visual Studies
Workshop (br). **20** Getty Images: John Pratt / Stringer (b). **21** Image courtesy of SRI International. (tr). **23** Alamy Stock Photo: allOver images. **24-25** ©Sony Corporation.
26 Alamy Stock Photo: Kathy deWitt (ca). **27** Getty Images: Raleigh News & Observer (tr). **28** Rex Shutterstock: Everett Kennedy Brown / EPA (cl). **29** 123RF.com: stefan
(cr). Dreamstime.com: Idn Idn (cla). **30** 123RF.com: Baloncici (cl). Piaggio Fast Forward: Ingo Meckmann (crb, bc). **31** Alamy Stock Photo: andrew chittock (br). Promo-
promo-bot.ru: (cla, cra). **33** Alamy Stock Photo: dpa picture alliance archive (l). **34-35** Intuitive Surgical, Inc.: © (2009) Intuitive Surgical, Inc. Used with permission. (b)
©Yaskawa America, Inc.: (b). **38** Courtesy of iRobot: (t). **39** Getty Images: YOSHIKAZU TSUNO / AFP (br). **41** Getty Images: Cate Gillon- With Permission From Mechatronics
www.mechatrons.com (t). **42-43** Teddy Seguin: Osada / Seguin / DRASSM (t). **44** NASA: JPL / Cornell University (t). **45** NASA: (b). **46-47** NASA: JPL-Caltech (b). **48-49** Alamy
Stock Photo: PJF Military Collection. **50** 123RF.com: jarp5 (cl). Courtesy of iRobot: (bc). **51** From/by Softbank Robotics: (l). NASA: Lora Koenig / NASA Goddard (cra). **51**
Engineered Arts Limited: (l). **54-55** Rethink Robotics: (b). **56-57** Getty Images: Yamaguchi Haruyoshi / Corbis (b). **58** Getty Images: YOSHIKAZU TSUNO / AFP (tr). **59** Alamy
Stock Photo: jeremy sutton-hibbert (cb). **60-61** From/by Softbank Robotics. **62-63** From/by Softbank Robotics. **64** Rex Shutterstock: James Gourley (r). **65** Rex Shutterstock:
James Gourley (clb); Ray Tang / LNP (crb). **66-67** www.poppy-project.org: Photo Equipe Flowers (b). **68** The Robot Studio. **70** NASA: (crb). NOAA: NOAA Okeanos Explorer
Program (cll). **71** NASA: JPL-Caltech / MSSS (cla); JPL-CalTech (bl). National Oceanography Centre, Southampton: (cra). **73** 123RF.com: Irina Alyakina (b). **74-75**
Consequential Robotics / Eaglemoss: (All Three Miro Robots). **76** Getty Images: Heritage Images (tc). **78** 123RF.com: georgejmclittle (tl). **79** Amazon.com, Inc.: (cl). **80**
Waymo: (b). **82** 123RF.com: Dmitry Azarov (t). **88** Alamy Stock Photo: SPUTNIK (c). Getty Images: Bettmann (cla); Science & Society Picture Library (clb). Rex Shutterstock:
Times Newspapers Ltd (cra). Science Photo Library: Peter Menzel (bc); Sam Ogden (crb). **89** Getty Images: Business Wire (tc); James Leynse (cl); Kathryn Scott Osler /
Harvard John A. Paulson School of Engineering and Applied Sciences: Lori Sanders / Harvard University (tr). NASA: (cra). Rex Shutterstock: (br). ©Sony Corporation: (cl).
91 Dorling Kindersley: Gary Ombler / International Robotics (br). Getty Images: Junko Kimura (bc)

Jacket images: Front: **123RF.com:** Kheng Ho Toh (Background); Dorling Kindersley: Geoff Brightling / Department of Electrical and Electronic Engineering, University of
Portsmouth tr, Gary Ombler / International Robotics tl; Getty Images: Junko Kimura crb, Kyodo News crb; Rex Shutterstock: James Gourley c; Back: **123RF.com:** Tatiana
Shepeleva cla; Dorling Kindersley: Gary Ombler / John Rigg, The Robot Hut cra

A WORLD OF IDEAS:
SEE ALL THERE IS TO KNOW

www.dk.com

Contents

Chapter 1
What is a robot?

The word "robot" makes most people think of a machine shaped like a metal human, like the ones you see in movies. In real life, robots come in many shapes and sizes. Some of the most powerful and complex robots do not look or behave anything like humans.

A robot is a machine that can do things automatically, or on its own. This might mean it can carry out a task by itself. Robots can also interact with the world around them. Modern robots are programmed to do different things using computers. They carry out jobs that humans can't do, such as lifting heavy objects. They also do jobs that humans don't want to do, because they are dangerous, dirty, or boring. Many robots work in places that humans can't, such as inside dangerous volcanoes and down in the deep sea.

Some robots are humanoid—or humanlike. Many of these robots have senses, such as sight, which makes them aware of their surroundings.

Today, robots help humans in factories and hospitals. We can even build toy robots at home, such as Meccanoids. Robots are everywhere!

A young boy with a Meccanoid G15 KS robot

Robots have fascinated people for centuries. It is no surprise that they are found in many books, movies, and TV shows. Fictional robots often have their own personalities. They are usually much more advanced than real robots.

The Iron Giant by Ted Hughes is a book about a giant metal robot from space. At first, he gets into trouble for eating metal machinery from a farm. The robot ends up protecting planet Earth against a supersized alien. Comic books about robots are also very popular. Japanese comic *Doraemon* describes the adventures of a time-traveling robotic cat.

The movie *Metropolis* was made in 1927. It stars a shiny humanoid that has been the model for many robots in movies since. Robots have been heroes, villains, and comedians on the big screen. They have been all shapes and sizes. Lots of movies, such as the animation *Robots* (2005), feature humanoids. *Big Hero 6* (2014) stars a robot that has a kind personality.

Many TV shows have featured robots, too. Part-robot aliens called Cybermen in *Doctor Who* have terrified viewers since the 1960s, when they first appeared.

Robots have captured the imagination of storytellers—and that does not look set to change any time soon!

The Cybermen are fictional villains.

Parts of a robot

Whatever their shape, size, or function, there are some parts that most robots have in common. These are the parts that make robots work.

Sensors
Sensors help a robot understand its environment. Sensors include cameras and temperature detectors.

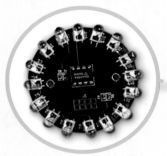

End effector
An end effector is a part that can be fitted where a robot's hand would be. Industrial robots can have grippers or welding torches as end effectors.

Nuts and bolts
Nuts and bolts hold different parts of a robot together.

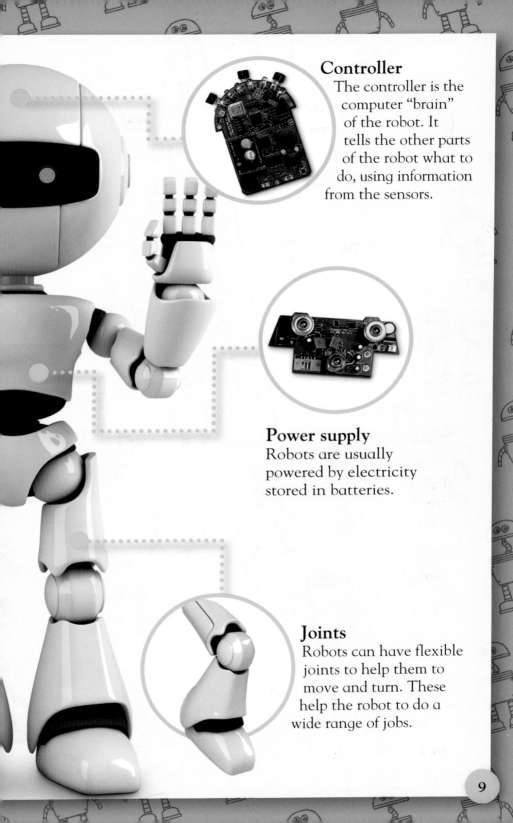

Controller

The controller is the computer "brain" of the robot. It tells the other parts of the robot what to do, using information from the sensors.

Power supply

Robots are usually powered by electricity stored in batteries.

Joints

Robots can have flexible joints to help them to move and turn. These help the robot to do a wide range of jobs.

Chapter 2
Early robots

Robots are often thought of as modern inventions, but robot-like machines have existed for more than two thousand years. The earliest examples of robots were automata, named so because they worked automatically.

In around 400 BCE, a mathematician in ancient Greece named Archytas is said to have built the first unpiloted "flying machine." It was a small wooden dove that flew a short distance.

Hero of Alexandria (10 CE–70 CE) was another

Hero of Alexandria created a machine that was powered by steam.

ancient Greek engineer who invented many automata. His work included singing birds, dancing figures, and models that poured water.

Ancient automata were our first attempts at robotic machines. However, these real-life inventions were not as awesome as some of the fictional robot-like beings in ancient myths. In one story, the Greek god Hephaestus made a giant bronze man named Talos, who protected Crete. A Chinese myth tells of the inventor Yan Shi. He is said to have created mechanical marvels such as a metal man who could walk, sing, and dance.

The mythical automaton Talos protected Crete from pirates.

Many wonderful automata were created during the Middle Ages, which lasted from the 5th century to the 15th century. These early robots often used clockwork to make them move. They would have appeared magical to people at the time.

In the 10th century, a man named Liutprand visited Constantinople, which is now Istanbul, in Turkey. He later wrote about the extraordinary machines he found at the imperial court. He described mechanical lions that roared and wagged their tails, bronze birds that sang in a tree, and a heavy throne that rose into the air.

About 200 years later, in 1206, an engineer named Ismail al-Jazari, from what is now Turkey, wrote a book called *The Book of Knowledge of Ingenious Mechanical Devices*.

The Book of Knowledge of Ingenious Mechanical Devices

It featured 100 mechanical devices, along with instructions on how to build many of them.

A boat with automatic musicians from
The Book of Knowledge of Ingenious Mechanical Devices

Ismail al-Jazari described a boat filled with robotic musicians that could play music for amazed guests. They could move in more than 50 different ways.

At the end of the Middle Ages, the famous Italian inventor and artist Leonardo da Vinci also designed automata. One of his designs was a humanoid knight that could sit up, turn its head, and move its arms.

Early robots were expensive. They were often used to show how rich their owners were. The lavish homes of French kings were full of fancy furniture, art, and, in some cases, automata. In the 17th century, as a child, King Louis XIV played with clever machines. An inventor named Camus is known to have made him a small moving coach with horses and footmen. It even had a tiny passenger that moved.

Automata were also built to entertain crowds. In 1737, the French engineer Jacques de Vaucanson created a flute player that moved and played music. It used artificial lungs to perform twelve songs. Another of Vaucanson's impressive inventions was a mechanical duck that seemed to eat, digest, and even poop! Jacques tricked viewers into thinking the food had been digested, when there was actually ready-made poop inside the duck.

In Japan, between the 17th and 19th centuries, mechanical puppets called karakuri were popular. Their name means "mechanisms" or "trick." The puppets were used in theaters and at religious festivals. Some were even used to serve tea at home.

You can still see examples of early automata today. 18th century Swiss inventor Henri Maillardet created one that could draw four pictures and write three poems. The model is now kept in the Franklin Institute Science Museum in Philadelphia.

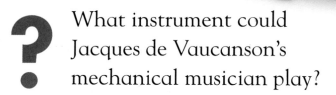

Japanese karakuri puppets could serve tea.

? What instrument could Jacques de Vaucanson's mechanical musician play?

Early robot inventors

For hundreds of years, imaginative inventors have created clockwork and robotic machines. Early mechanical animals and automata were far ahead of their times!

Archytas

In 400 BCE, this ancient Greek inventor was busy creating steam-powered wonders. His awesome inventions included a flying wooden bird!

Ismail al-Jazari

This Islamic engineer wrote a book called *The Book of Knowledge of Ingenious Mechanical Devices*, in 1206. It described 100 mechanical marvels.

Leonardo da Vinci

Da Vinci was an Italian inventor who used his genius to create hundreds of amazing machines. In 1495 he designed a robot knight.

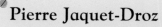
Pierre Jaquet-Droz

Swiss watchmaker Jaquet-Droz created three doll-like automata to display watches in the late 1700s.

Thomas de Colmar

In 1820, this French inventor created the first calculator. It was called the arithmometer. It could add, subtract, divide, and multiply numbers.

Chapter 3
Developments in robotics

In the 18th century, machines that made things such as cotton thread were invented. People started working in factories that were full of machines. They made sure that the machines didn't go wrong. This period of history was called the Industrial Revolution.

People realized that machines could do lots of jobs that were previously done by humans. The Jacquard loom was a machine invented in 1804. It could weave patterns in fabric by following instructions on a card punched with holes.

The Jacquard loom could weave complicated patterns in fabric.

The machine took on human tasks, but looked nothing like the people who worked alongside it.

The word "robot" first appeared in 1920 in a play by Czech writer Karel Capek. It means "slave." Robots became common in books and movies. People were fascinated by the idea that these clever machines could one day become part of everyday life.

By the 1920s, robotic machines started to look more like humans and were much more impressive than early automata. These were called humanoid robots. In 1939, a robot named Elektro appeared at the World's Fair. He was 6.5 ft (2 m) tall, had aluminum skin, and could talk. Soon, robots would be able to do much more.

Elektro singing at the 1939 New York World's Fair.

In 1948, William Grey Walter invented the first robotic animal that could move around independently. He named it Elmer. It had bump sensors, which detected things that the robot knocked into. It could explore its environment like a real animal. When it reached an obstacle, it could move around it without being told to. The slow way it moved led to it being called a tortoise. Walter created a friend for Elmer, named Elsie. These clever tortoises could find their way

William Grey Walter with one of his tortoise robots, Elmer

to a charging station when they ran low on battery power.

Between 1966 and 1972, scientists at Stanford Research Institute developed a robot named Shakey. It wobbled when it moved. It had bump sensors at its base, and a television camera in its head that allowed it to see. Shakey could figure out routes through a series of rooms using its robotic senses of sight and touch. Shakey could also communicate. Commands could be typed into the robot's computer, and it would type back an answer.

Shakey

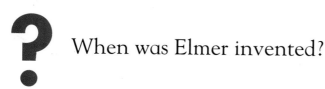

? When was Elmer invented?

People decided to see if they could create robots that were smart enough to play games against humans. In 1996, a computer called Deep Blue played the world chess champion Garry Kasparov, but lost. The next year, having been upgraded, it successfully defeated Kasparov. Deep Blue could consider an amazing 200 million chess positions every second.

In June 1993, a group of Japanese researchers launched a robot soccer competition. It was called the Robot World Cup Initiative, or "RoboCup" for short. The goal of RoboCup is to create a robot team that can beat a team made up of the world's best human soccer players by the year 2050. This is no easy task. For example, the two-legged robots created so far are much slower than human soccer players.

The first RoboCup games took place in Japan in 1997, with more than 40 teams taking part. By 2015, more than 500 teams were taking part, from more than 45 different countries. The robots vary in size from small, mug-sized creations to adult-sized robots.

A robot soccer player in the 2009 RoboCup games

In movies and television shows, robotic pets make some of the best companions. The robotic dog K9 in the TV series *Doctor Who* can talk and has a laser weapon built into his nose. He is also more intelligent than most humans!

In the late 1990s and early 2000s, a variety of fun robotic pets were invented in real life. First, the Japanese company Sony released AIBO, a robotic dog. The word "aibo" means partner, or pal, in Japanese.

The next year saw the arrival of Tekno the Robotic Puppy. More than 40 million Tekno puppies were sold in its first four years. It had an impressive 160 emotions and functions, including barking, walking, and sleeping. Light sensors in some models meant the dog could respond to things it could see. It could be trained like a real dog to react to voice commands and to do tricks, such as playing fetch. In the future, robotic pets may become even more realistic.

Some robotic dogs don't just copy animals, but take on new behaviors. SpotMini is a recently-developed robot dog that can help clean around the house by picking up objects. The future of robotic pets could involve intelligent creatures that can talk to us, just like in movies.

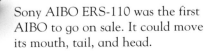

Sony AIBO ERS-110 was the first AIBO to go on sale. It could move its mouth, tail, and head.

The idea of combining a human and a machine is not a new one. The word "cyborg" was coined during the 1960s. It is short for "cybernetic organism," which means a living thing with mechanical parts.

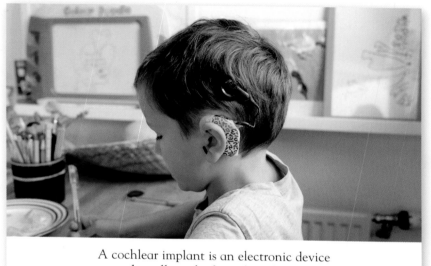

A cochlear implant is an electronic device that allows deaf people to hear!

Cyborgs only exist in science fiction movies, but mechanical parts have been used to help people with medical problems. For example, an artificial pacemaker is a small machine placed inside the bodies of people with heart problems, to help their hearts work properly. Tiny devices are also being developed that will hopefully go inside the brain to help some blind people to see.

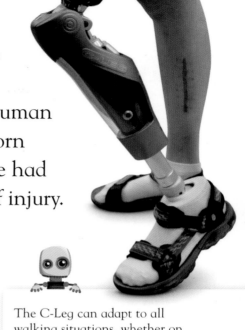

Perhaps the most amazing developments are robotic limbs. These have been designed to replace human arms and legs for people born without limbs, or who have had them amputated because of injury. The C-Leg, for example, is controlled by a computer circuit, which tells it what to do. Its knee joint is controlled by sensors that detect uneven ground to help the user walk on different surfaces.

The C-Leg can adapt to all walking situations, whether on level ground, stairs, or ramps.

In 2001, American Jesse Sullivan became the first person to operate a robotic limb using his brain. He lost his arms after an accident at work, in which he received a huge electric shock. Soon after his accident at work, scientists replaced his left arm with a robotic arm. Jesse's thoughts control the movements of his robotic arm by sending signals from his brain along rerouted nerves that are attached to the arm.

Machine power

Machines are powered in lots of different ways. Early machines used clockwork, steam, and pulley systems to operate. These days, robots usually run on rechargeable batteries.

Clockwork automata

Early machines often used clockwork. This is a system of metal cogs and wheels that turn, making different parts of the machines move.

A robot that has a clockwork mechanism

An engine that runs on steam

Battery-powered machines

Modern machines mostly use batteries to power them. Batteries create electricity using chemicals. Machines use this electricity to move.

A robotic lawn mower powered by batteries

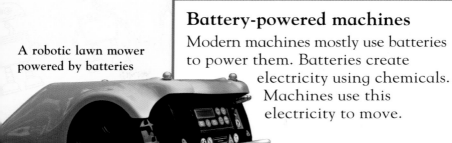

Hydraulic machines

Hydraulic machines use water or other liquids, pushed through tubes, to make parts move. Many of today's vehicles have hydraulic systems.

A bulldozer that uses a hydraulic system

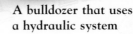

Steam-powered machines

In early tractors and trains, water was heated until it turned to steam. This steam was used to power the machine.

Types of robot

Today, there are many different types of robot. From robots in factories to military machines, robots are helping people in lots of ways.

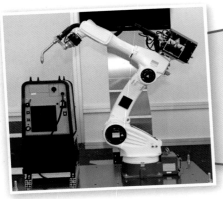

Stationary robots

Robots that stay in one place to do their jobs are called "stationary robots." Most factory robots are stationary.

A stationary robotic arm used in factories

Mobile robots

Mobile robots can move around to carry, lift, and search for things. They may run on wheels or have legs.

Gita is a robot that carries things.

Metrosha interacts with passengers at a metro station in Moscow, Russia.

Autonomous robots

Some robots can decide how to do things themselves. They are autonomous, which means they can run without the help of a human.

Remote-controlled robots

Remote-controlled robots are guided by a human operator. They can perform difficult or dangerous tasks without the need for a human to be present.

Dragon Runner is used by the US military.

Chapter 4
Robots everywhere

Today, humans use robots in lots of different ways. They are more sophisticated than ever before. Think for a moment about all the things that different robots do every day.

Factories are full of robots helping to build all sorts of things, from computers to cars. Drones, which are a type of flying robot, are used to deliver mail, and to film incredible footage for television shows and movies from the skies.

Robots entertain us in museums. They can be designed to look and act like dinosaurs from millions of years ago. They act as our pets, and can look after us when we are old. They have been developed to help rescue us from danger after accidents and disasters.

They carry out dangerous and difficult work to examine the mysterious world at the bottom of the oceans. They are also used in military operations and on space missions.

Robots are transforming transportation. Self-driving cars, trains, and buses are being developed. In the future, people might not ever need to drive cars themselves. It is hard to imagine a world without robots!

This humanoid robot, HRP-2 Promet, can figure out ways of moving heavy objects on its own.

Medical robots help save lives by improving how people are treated for illnesses. Some robots are used in operations. Others can identify illnesses, perform blood tests, or help care for people who are ill or recovering after treatment.

The Da Vinci System is a surgical robot that helps surgeons perform complicated operations. Surgical robots can be used remotely. This means a surgeon can operate without being in the same room as the patient. Remote surgery can save lives by connecting doctors to patients quickly.

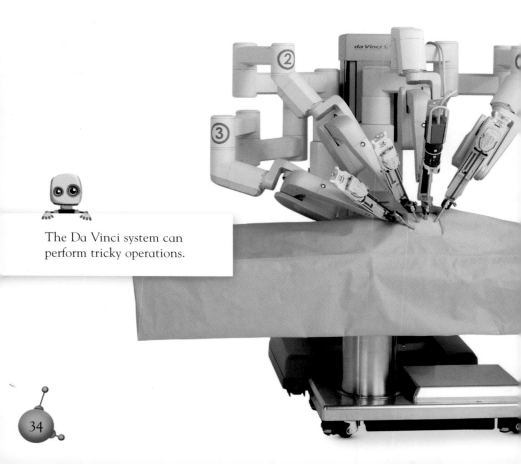

The Da Vinci system can perform tricky operations.

Surgical robots help surgeons make smaller cuts when they open people up to operate on them. The patient will heal faster and lose less blood. They will also have less pain and scarring, and they can go home sooner.

Other medical robots include the ViRob and RIBA. The ViRob is a tiny robot that can diagnose illnesses and send images from inside the body. At just 0.04 in (1 mm) long, it is small enough to crawl inside veins. The RIBA is a

robotic healthcare assistant, shaped like a bear. It can lift and move patients. This is safer for healthcare workers since it avoids risking back injuries. It is also more comforting for patients to be lifted by a RIBA than by a mechanical hoist.

Industrial robots are used in factories to make things. They can be programmed to carry out tasks that are dangerous, heavy, boring, or dirty, so that humans do not need to do them. Different types of robot can be programmed to handle, join, paint, carry, and move things. They can also assemble, package, and label things.

The way industrial robots look and how they are built depends on the jobs they are designed

Motoman SDA10 is designed to build complicated things.

to do. Painting robots need to have lots of joints, so they can move into many positions to paint things. Assembly robots are built to make the precise and fast repeated movements needed to put things together.

Unlike humans, robots never get bored, tired, or sick. They can work non-stop. They work quickly and accurately, and they do not need breaks. The replacement of human workers by machines is called mechanization, and it has meant that there is less work for people to do in factories.

By the end of this century, robots will have changed the way we work just as dramatically. Jobs for assembly line workers, warehouse workers, machine cleaners, and many other types of worker will disappear. Humans will not be out of work though. Robots will free them to be creative and find new ways of working.

? How are robots better workers than humans?

This robot vacuum cleaner, the Roomba, can clean floors all on its own.

Service jobs, such as cleaning, mowing grass, and delivering goods, can now be done by robots. There are also security robots programmed to help keep us safe from harm.

Service robots carry out useful tasks for humans in an independent way. The Roomba is a robot vacuum cleaner, introduced in 2002, programmed to clean by itself. It uses sensors to recognize dirt and clean it up. Sensors also let it move around. When it senses that things are in its path, the Roomba can change direction. It can also sense steps so that it does not fall down them. It can sense dirt on the floor and clean it up.

There are many other service robots. The Scooba washes floors, the Dressman irons clothes, and the Looj cleans out gutters. Kitchen robots, such as a robotic chef, are being developed. Larger cleaning robots, such as the Hydrobot, are used in schools, hospitals, and factories. They clean huge spaces quickly—10,000 ft² (930 m²) per hour!

Security robots are used to patrol areas, keeping them safe. They monitor activity and detect movement and intruders, and can send alerts for help. They can take video footage, and store and share it. The Guardrobo D1 was designed to patrol stores and offices in Japan. It can even put out fires.

Guardrobo D1 can send camera footage or contact people by radio if there is a fire or a break-in.

Robots entertain us, and give us pleasure. Many theme park rides, movies, museums, exhibitions, and art shows now use robots.

In 1963, an attraction called Walt Disney's Enchanted Tiki Room opened in the Disneyland theme park in California. Nothing had been seen like it before, anywhere in the world. It featured more than 150 talking, singing, and dancing birds and flowers. They were controlled by a room full of computers. In 2005, the Tiki Room was refurbished for the park's 50th anniversary. Completely new animatronic figures—robots with lifelike features—were made.

In 1964, *Mary Poppins* was the first movie to feature animatronic characters—two robins. Animatronics have now been creating exciting special effects in movies for decades. In 1993, the Stan Winston Studio created an animatronic Tyrannosaurus rex for the movie *Jurassic Park*. It was the largest animatronic figure ever made. It weighed 6.6 tons (6 metric tons) and was 20 ft (6 m) tall and 40 ft (12 m) long to the tip of its tail. It moved and roared, bringing dinosaurs to life for moviegoers.

RuBot II solved the Rubik's Cube in less than half a minute.

Robots have even been made to solve the Rubik's Cube puzzle. In 2010, the RuBot II, nicknamed "The Cubinator," took 21 seconds to solve the puzzle. By 2017, a robot named Sub1 Reloaded had solved it in under one second!

The deep sea is the least explored place on Earth. It reaches thousands of feet deep in some areas, and humans can't survive at those depths without very expensive crafts to keep them safe. Robots don't need air and won't be crushed by the weight of thousands of tons of water above them.

Underwater robots find out about the amazing creatures that live in the deep. They can film and take photos. They can also be used to build, repair, and retrieve things in the ocean. Some work independently, while others are controlled by people from a distance.

OceanOne is a mermaid-like robot that swims down to the seabed without needing to come up for air. It can dive much deeper than a human and delicately take samples of old shipwrecks with its humanlike hands. OceanOne doesn't

OceanOne is an underwater humanoid robot that lets scientists explore the depths of the oceans.

work on its own, but is controlled by a human. The controller can feel the weight of things held by the robot. This creates a hands-on experience.

Uncrewed underwater vehicles are sent out to explore the ocean without people controlling them. They can swim across oceans, recording data such as temperature. This tells scientists how climate change is affecting the ocean. At the end of their missions, they return with data to the scientists who sent them out.

NASA's Mars Exploration rovers were sent to the Red Planet to study rocks and soils.

Robots and space seem to go together perfectly—and not just because of science fiction movies like *Star Wars*! Robots can explore, investigate, and carry out tasks in this hostile environment, where there is no air and temperatures are deadly.

Uncrewed robotic spacecraft can travel farther in space than spacecraft crewed with humans. They are also cheaper than human space travel and mean that astronauts don't need to go on dangerous missions. They can even explore planets such as Jupiter, Mars, and Venus.

The accurate data and images they send back to Earth allow scientists to learn about these mysterious landscapes.

Robotic explorers often take the form of driverless spacecraft or vehicles. The Mars Exploration rovers are vehicles controlled by onboard computers.

Robonaut is a robot created by NASA. It will work just like a human astronaut in space—or even better. Work on the first Robonaut started in 1996. The latest version was built on the International Space Station in 2011. The robot has a five-fingered hand and human-style arm with 150 sensors. It can use tools developed for astronauts. Scientists can give Robonaut tasks, and its computer figures out how to do them. The robot can also be run by remote control.

Robonaut is the first space humanoid.

People in the emergency services, such as firemen, will often risk their lives to save others by running into burning houses or collapsed mining tunnels. Rescue robots are designed to get people to safety after disasters and explosions so that human rescuers don't have to put themselves in danger. These robots are strong enough to go into dangerous places and come out again without much damage. They can also get to difficult places that humans can't.

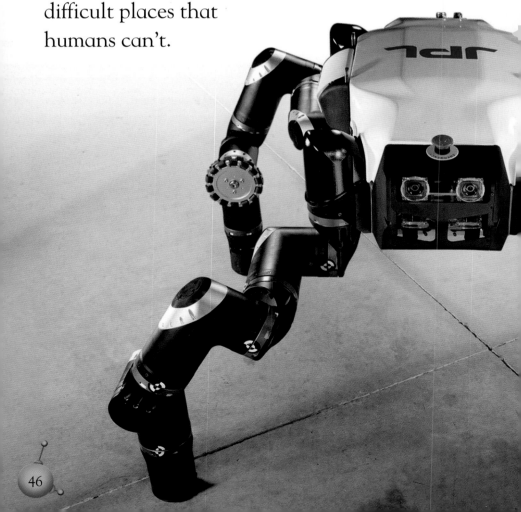

Rescue robots were used after the collapse of the World Trade Center in New York City in 2001. They looked for victims and survivors in the rubble. They found the rough ground difficult, and some got stuck and were damaged. Scientists learned from this and are trying to improve their designs. Daniel Goldman at Georgia Tech is looking at animals for new ideas. He is developing a rescue robot that burrows through rubble like a sandfish lizard. This will make it easier for the robot to reach people trapped under rubble.

Robots are being developed to use special equipment to search for survivors. They will create maps of dangerous areas and deliver medical treatment to victims.

RoboSimian has been designed to rescue people in places hit by disasters.

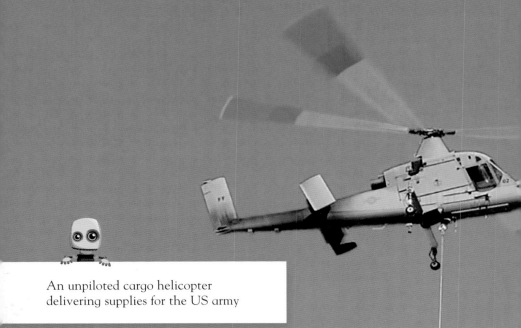

An unpiloted cargo helicopter
delivering supplies for the US army

Robots might one day be used in place of human soldiers, so that people won't ever need to go into battle. Today, military robots are already used in some military operations, such as delivering supplies.

Human soldiers often control military robots, but they can also be autonomous. The Snowgoose CQ-10 is a powered glider that has no pilot, and no human controlling it from a distance. It can carry up to 600 lb (262 kg) of supplies such as food, fuel, water, medical supplies, and ammunition to soldiers in remote and dangerous areas. Robotic vehicles on the ground are being designed to act as uncrewed ambulances, which could save the lives of injured soldiers.

In some war zones, enemy bombs are planted in the ground and pose a threat to soldiers and civilians. Military robots save the day by carrying out bomb-disposal tasks. They can also detect enemy soldiers hidden from human view. This means that soldiers working alongside the robots can avoid being attacked in dangerous areas.

Unpiloted robotic aircraft, called drones, are also used to drop bombs. Many people protest against military robots that can kill people. Groups such as Human Rights Watch have campaigned to stop their development. In 2015, more than 1,000 experts in robotics signed a letter calling for a ban.

How robots move

Robots move in different ways according to the jobs they need to do. They may have legs, wheels, treads, or even rotors!

Drones can be used for aerial photography.

Rotors
Some robots can fly. They are called drones and have rotors. Drones are used to film from the sky or even to deliver packages to people.

Wheels
Many robots move on wheels. Wheels are stable, cheap, and strong, and can travel a long way without problems.

iRobot Mirra cleans swimming pools.

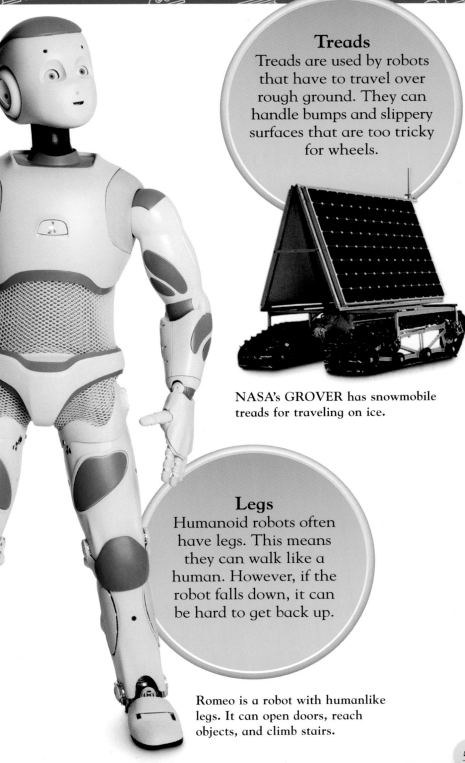

Treads
Treads are used by robots that have to travel over rough ground. They can handle bumps and slippery surfaces that are too tricky for wheels.

NASA's GROVER has snowmobile treads for traveling on ice.

Legs
Humanoid robots often have legs. This means they can walk like a human. However, if the robot falls down, it can be hard to get back up.

Romeo is a robot with humanlike legs. It can open doors, reach objects, and climb stairs.

51

Chapter 5
Humanoids

Science fiction movie-makers have been fascinated with the idea of a perfectly humanlike robot for many years. Now, they are starting to become a reality.

Humanoid robots are built to look and act like humans. The most realistic humanoid robots have a body, head, arms, and legs. Others are built from the waist upward. Humanoids often have electronic senses, such as sight and touch. Twendy-One is a humanoid developed in Japan. It has fingers so sensitive that it can pick up a coin from a flat surface.

Other humanoids have realistic faces. The robotic newsreader Kodomoroid was introduced in Tokyo, Japan, in 2014. It has soft artificial skin that makes it look like a real human.

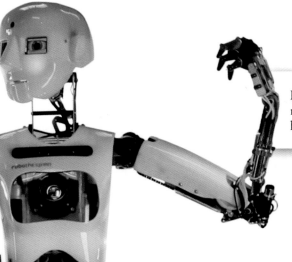

RoboThespian is a humanoid robot designed to interact with humans on a public platform.

Humanoid robots are used in different ways. They can do dangerous jobs, such as explore space. They can use their hands and arms to lift things, which means humans don't have to do boring tasks like stacking boxes. Other humanoid robots are created to help look after elderly people.

Some robots even mimic the way the human body works to make them move in a more human way. These robots have skeletons and muscles to help them move.

In the future, humans may need to work alongside robots in lots of different jobs. Most industrial robots today look like giant mechanical arms and work on their own. Baxter is a humanoid industrial robot that works beside human workers—it even communicates with them. Baxter is popular with its fellow workers because it takes on boring tasks so they don't have to!

Baxter was introduced by the US company Rethink Robotics in 2012. It is 3 ft (1 m) tall. It has two arms and can load objects onto tables, sort items into groups, and move things from one place to another.

Baxter's "face" is a digital screen that can show different expressions. For example, Baxter will look confused if something is not right. The robot has sensors around its head that help it to detect when people are nearby. This means Baxter is safe to be around since it won't accidentally bump into people. It also knows if it drops a tool, thanks to sensors in its hands, and can pick the tool up again.

Baxter can even learn new tasks when it is shown how to do them, almost like a human.

Baxter uses its vision to locate and grasp objects with its flexible grippers.

You might accidentally mistake the Actroid for a real human. This amazingly lifelike robot is designed to look like a young Japanese woman. It was first revealed in 2003 at the International Robot Exhibition in Japan.

Each Actroid robot has realistic skin made out of a soft rubber material, called silicone. Actroids can talk and blink. The latest models even move their chest as if they are breathing. The Actroid can listen to words and answer in a natural way when it is spoken to.

Kodomoroid (*left*) and Otonaroid (*right*) are the world's first android newscasters.

An Actroid can learn how to move like a human. It does this by facing a person who is marked with reflective dots on points around their body. It then tracks the dots with its sensors. The Actroid moves to match the movements it sees. It can then repeat the movements that it has learned.

In 2014, the Actroid's developer introduced the Kodomoroid—a news-reading humanoid robot. It delivered news of an earthquake to stunned onlookers in Tokyo.

Humanoids are perfect for the home because they fit in with the rest of the human-shaped family. Lots of companies have started to develop humanoids for the home, but one practical robot came first.

The Wakamaru robot was first shown to the world in 2005. It was made by the Japanese company Mitsubishi and

Wakamaru can identify people using its voice and face-recognition system.

has a humanlike shape, although it is yellow and only 3 ft (1 m) tall. Wakamaru has arms and moves around on wheels. It has special sensors to stop it from bumping into things, which helps to make it safe around humans.

Wakamaru was developed to help humans, particularly elderly and disabled people. It can recognize 10,000 words and eight human faces. It can also find people using heat and sound sensors. It was designed to learn the daily routines of people in their homes and can call outside for help in an emergency.

Wakamaru can only work in single-story buildings because of its wheel base. It is also very expensive. Wakamaru cost over $14,000 when it went on sale in 2005, which meant that not many people could afford one! Robots are getting cheaper as technology advances, which means we might all have a house robot one day.

Wakamaru interacting with a young boy

Interactive companion robots are designed to be robo-friends that we can spend time with. NAO is one of the best examples of this kind of robot. In 2015, it also competed in the RoboCup— the robot soccer World Cup!

NAO was first developed in 2004 by SoftBank Robotics. It is child-sized and 23 in (58 cm) tall. NAO can speak 14 languages and recognize emotions. The robot can tell different faces apart and has four microphones that act as ears.

NAO is used to teach students how to program robots to do different things. Students can also use NAO to study the way humans and robots interact with each other.

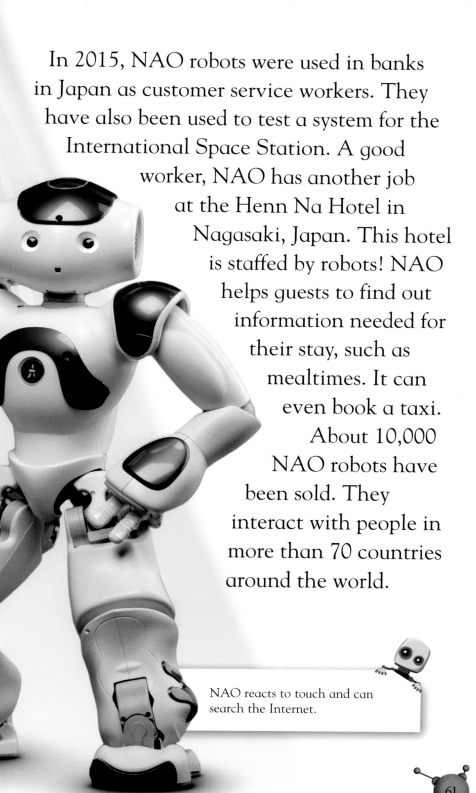

In 2015, NAO robots were used in banks in Japan as customer service workers. They have also been used to test a system for the International Space Station. A good worker, NAO has another job at the Henn Na Hotel in Nagasaki, Japan. This hotel is staffed by robots! NAO helps guests to find out information needed for their stay, such as mealtimes. It can even book a taxi. About 10,000 NAO robots have been sold. They interact with people in more than 70 countries around the world.

NAO reacts to touch and can search the Internet.

While we'd all like to have a robot friend, they might be most useful to elderly people who find it hard to leave their homes. Companion robots could help them remember to do things and help them to get around. A robot could also be someone to talk to if people can't go and visit their friends.

The Romeo robot was first developed in 2009. It was designed to be a companion and helper for elderly people in their homes. Romeo is 4.6 ft (1.4 m) tall and can open doors, climb stairs, and move objects. Romeo makes sure people are safe and well, and can detect if someone has had a fall. It can also remind people to take their medicine and to go to upcoming appointments. It will even introduce people in a retirement home to each other to help them make friends. Romeo can help people feel less lonely in more than one way!

Romeo's developers are now trying to teach the robot to learn. If they can do this, it will know what people need by their actions. For example, if an elderly person sits down to watch television, Romeo could offer them their glasses. Romeo is also being taught to make pancakes—using a recipe it has downloaded from the Internet.

Romeo could one day help elderly people feel independent, since they won't need to rely on human help.

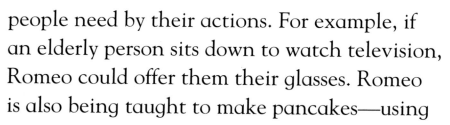
Romeo can move its eyes and stand on two legs like a human.

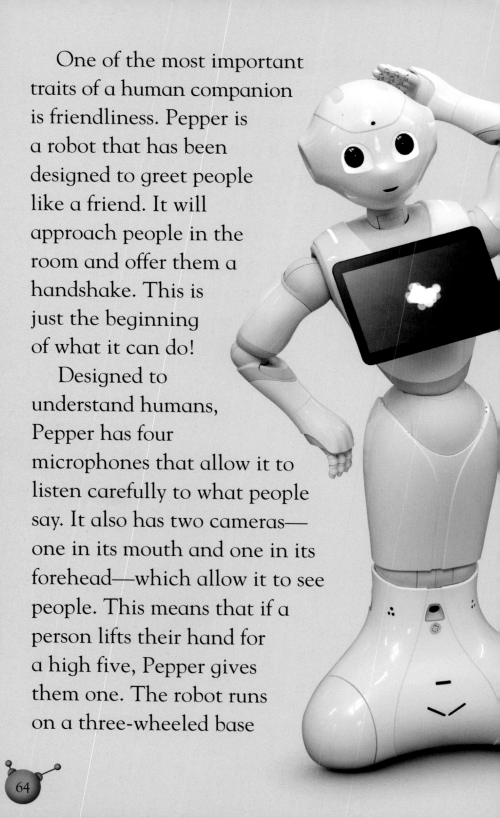

One of the most important traits of a human companion is friendliness. Pepper is a robot that has been designed to greet people like a friend. It will approach people in the room and offer them a handshake. This is just the beginning of what it can do!

Designed to understand humans, Pepper has four microphones that allow it to listen carefully to what people say. It also has two cameras— one in its mouth and one in its forehead—which allow it to see people. This means that if a person lifts their hand for a high five, Pepper gives them one. The robot runs on a three-wheeled base and knows when people are nearby so it doesn't bump into them.

Pepper was created purely to make people happy. It is designed to help people have fun. Each Pepper robot uploads its experiences with humans to a storage system on the Internet. Other Pepper units can then download the experiences and learn from them. This helps Pepper to learn quickly how to act more like a human.

"Nice to meet you."

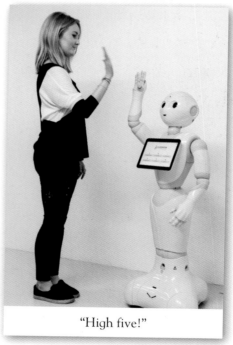

"High five!"

You no longer need to be a specialist engineer to build an advanced humanoid robot! Poppy is an open source humanoid robot. This means that the materials and plans to build the robot have been made available on the Internet for anyone to use. Even the computer codes that instruct it to move can be found online.

To make the robot, people can download the plans for parts, and print them out using a 3-D printer. Poppy can then be put together in seven hours. It can be programmed by its builder to do different things, such as dance. It is used in schools and universities to learn about and experiment with robots. It is also used to study topics such as engineering.

A European project called KERAAL is using Poppy to develop a way to help patients with back pain. The robot is being developed as an assistant to help patients with their exercises. Poppy will demonstrate the exercises, showing the most important parts of each movement. The robot will then watch patients with its camera, and examine their movements in detail. It can then tell the patients if they are doing the exercises in the right way!

The Poppy Torso is a variation of the Poppy humanoid robot. It can be easily installed on tabletops.

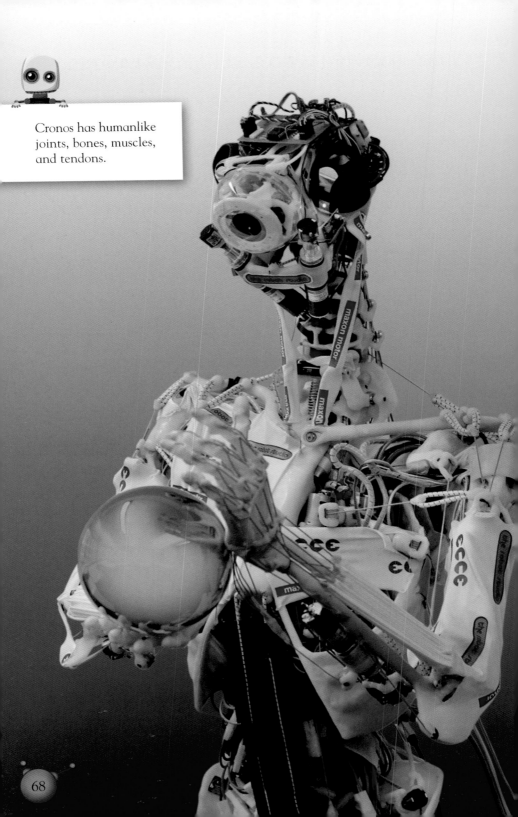

Cronos has humanlike joints, bones, muscles, and tendons.

Human bodies have complicated systems that help them function. The brain and nervous system help us think and feel. Muscles and tendons pull on different bones to make our bodies move.

Some scientists think that robots can become more humanlike if they copy the way our bodies work. Eccerobot has elastic parts that resemble muscles and tendons. These are attached to an artificial skeleton. The muscles pull on different parts of the skeleton to allow it to move.

Cronos is another robot with a skeleton and elastic muscles. The muscles inside Cronos have been copied almost exactly from the human body's muscular system. It has a long, flexible neck and spine, and movable wrists and hands. Roboy is a childlike version of a muscular robot. Roboy's developers are trying to make its legs strong enough to ride a bike.

These developments in robotics are creating robots that can move like humans rather than stiff machines. However, there is still a long way to go before the human body is recreated in a machine.

Robotic explorers

Robots can explore uncomfortable and remote places that are too dangerous for human explorers. They can travel deep under the sea and even work in space.

Deep Discoverer
This ocean-going robot explores the seabed. In 2016, it discovered a new species of deep-sea octopus.

Valkyrie
This humanoid robot has been designed to work in space. Scientists hope it will one day help astronauts on Mars.

Curiosity rover

This space exploration robot is stationed on Mars. It sends data back to Earth, including incredible photos of the Martian surface.

Autosub3

Autosub3 is a self-controlling submarine that can map the seabed. It has explored under Antarctic sea ice.

VolcanoBot1

This amazing robot collects data from inside volcanoes—warning scientists about possible eruptions.

Chapter 6
What is Artificial Intelligence?

Lots of the robots in this book are smart, but do they have humanlike intelligence? Artificial intelligence, or AI, is what scientists call the ability of robots to "think" in a similar way to humans. The term was first used in 1955, by the computer scientist John McCarthy.

Humans learn by experience. If you touch something sharp, it pricks your finger and hurts. Next time you see something sharp, you know not to touch it, because you have learned from your experience. This learning process is the key to intelligence. People can decide what to do in new situations because of things they have learned in the past.

Scientists are working to create special programs that help robots to think. They are trying to create robots that can apply the knowledge that they collect to new skills and situations. AI allows robot-thinking to develop and get better, just like human intelligence.

Machines can already store a huge amount of information and use it to work out the answers to questions or commands quickly. Labs run by companies such as Microsoft, Google, and Facebook are hard at work developing brand-new and exciting AI technology.

Robots with AI can beat humans at chess by considering thousands of different moves.

MiRo is a biomimetic robot. This means that the robot's design is based on a living thing. Its creators at the University of Sheffield in the UK have tried to build a robot that thinks like an animal—and looks like a cute dog.

MiRo has lots of sensors that help it to act like a living thing. It can detect movement, so it will approach people like a real dog. It will also wag its tail if it is stroked behind its ears.

MiRo is designed to help care for elderly or disabled people at home. Having a lifelike companion is important so that people don't get lonely. The robot can be programmed to look for changes in a person's routine. Sensors within the home would detect if a person had fallen down, and alert MiRo. The dog would then go to investigate.

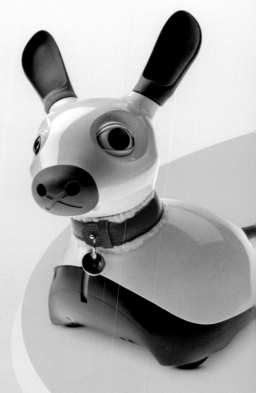

It would talk to the person, to see if they were OK. If it didn't get an answer, it could call a human caregiver for help.

MiRo can recharge itself, so it could look after a human independently. It could turn out to be the best pet ever!

MiRo can make decisions, sense its surroundings, and respond to its owner.

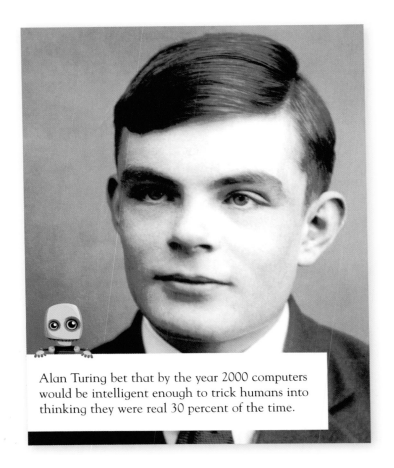

Alan Turing bet that by the year 2000 computers would be intelligent enough to trick humans into thinking they were real 30 percent of the time.

Alan Turing was an English mathematician who created a test for artificial intelligence in 1950. It is still used by scientists today. They call it the Turing Test.

In the test, a person is put in a room and asked to talk to two voices. One is a computer and the other is a human. They are all in separate rooms, so they can't see each other.

The person asks questions and then decides which voice belongs to the human and which belongs to the computer, based on the way each one answers. If the person asking the questions can't tell, the machine is seen to be intelligent.

Some scientists believe we need a new and more complicated test. American psychologist Gary Marcus says that we need a variety of tests to look for artificial intelligence from different viewpoints. This is because humans have very complex brains and high intelligence.

Dartmouth College in New Hampshire has a special competition that asks machines to write poems, short stories, music, and more. So far, this competition has not found a robot that can pass as a human writer—but time will tell!

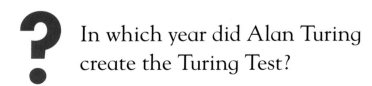

? In which year did Alan Turing create the Turing Test?

Most of today's smartphones have a virtual personal assistant.

Artificial intelligence is used every day, by millions of people around the world, without them really thinking about it! Many mobile devices, such as phones, tablets, and smartwatches, use AI software, which means you can ask them questions and receive an answer.

Siri is software that acts as a virtual personal assistant. It runs on Apple devices, such as iPhones and iPads. A person using Siri can talk to the program. It recognizes the words spoken and can respond. Its artificial intelligence allows it to adapt to the person using it, making it better at recognizing the words a person uses over time. It also learns the types of things a user searches for.

Amazon's Alexa is another virtual assistant that does things for its owner. Users can talk to Alexa, asking questions and giving commands to play music or even order takeout food. These clever devices can even switch on lights that have special "smart" technology in your home. This technology allows the

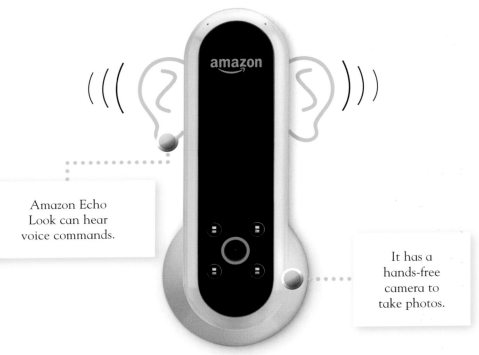

Amazon Echo Look can hear voice commands.

It has a hands-free camera to take photos.

Amazon Echo Look is one of the Alexa-enabled devices.

lights to connect to the Internet, which Alexa uses to control them. As more smart devices are invented, Alexa could be able to control many more things around the home.

Robots seem perfectly suited to driving long distances because they don't get tired! However, driving requires people to constantly adapt to new situations—such as traffic jams or diversions. Robot cars would need to be very aware of their surroundings and able to make decisions on how to act in new situations.

Google began a self-driving car project called Waymo in 2009. In 2014, the company had invented a car with no steering wheel, and no pedals to make the car stop or go faster. By 2015, the car was being tested on roads.

Each Waymo car uses a laser to create a 3-D map of its surroundings. The onboard computer system uses this map, combined with digital maps of the area, to drive the car. The car drives at the speed limit, and it stays at the right distance behind other cars, using sensors that detect how far away they are.

Self-driving cars could help people who are unable to drive because of physical difficulties or old age. They're the cars of the future!

Waymo self-driving cars have driven more than 3 million miles (5 million km).

Nanobots are robots so small that they can only be seen under a microscope.

Robot technology is advancing fast. Artificial intelligence is becoming a reality, and robots are part of everyday life. So, what does the future hold?

Ray Kurzweil, a director of engineering at Google, thinks that by the 2030s, humans will have nanobots—tiny robots—implanted in their brains. He says that this technology will allow us to connect to the Internet using our brains. This would mean we could receive information directly when we need it. He says we could also transfer information from our brains onto an online storage space, called the cloud, so nothing would ever be lost or forgotten.

Our strength may be about to increase, too, thanks to robotics. Technology is being developed to provide special suits and clothes to add to the strength of a human. The Swedish company BioServo has invented a robotic glove for people with a weak grip, perhaps due to injury. They are now developing a new glove that will make the wearer's grip even stronger, using space technology from NASA and engineering from car company General Motors.

In all areas of our lives—health, education, work, and at home—robots are being used to make life easier and better for humans. Whatever the future holds, robots will be there!

Robot learning

Robots can be taught to do things. Humans learn by doing things and being shown how to do them better. Some robots can do this, too!

1. Training
Baxter the robot is trained by a person. It can be taught how to use its gripper to pick up objects.

2. Trial and error

Baxter tries to pick up different-shaped objects with its grippers, but at the start keeps dropping them!

3. Starting to learn

By repeating the process, Baxter learns how to lift the objects. It stores this information for the next time.

Inventing a robot

To invent a robot, you have to think carefully about what you want it to do and how it will do it. What sort of robot would be able to rescue a cat from a tree?

1

Purpose

To design a robot, you first need to think about what it is for. Your purpose here is to solve the problem of a cat stuck up in a tree.

2

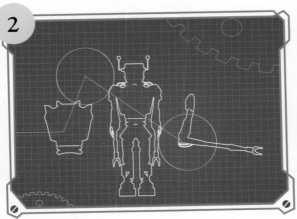

Functionality

Next, think about the job the robot needs to do. It needs to be able to reach, fly, or climb to high places, before carrying the cat safely to the ground.

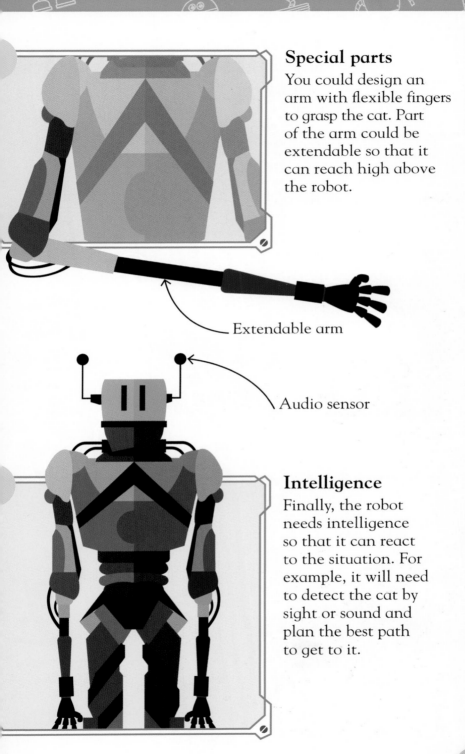

Special parts

You could design an arm with flexible fingers to grasp the cat. Part of the arm could be extendable so that it can reach high above the robot.

Extendable arm

Audio sensor

Intelligence

Finally, the robot needs intelligence so that it can react to the situation. For example, it will need to detect the cat by sight or sound and plan the best path to get to it.

Robots through time

From rovers to robotic dogs, here are some of the key developments in the history of robots.

1739
A mechanical duck is created by Jacques de Vaucanson.

1970
Lunokhod 1, a Soviet rover, explores the Moon.

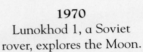

1989
AGV HelpMate takes supplies around a hospital

1961
Unimate, the first industrial robot, helps to make cars.

1973
WABOT-1, a human-sized robot, is introduced.

1998
The Kismet robot displays reactions and emotions.

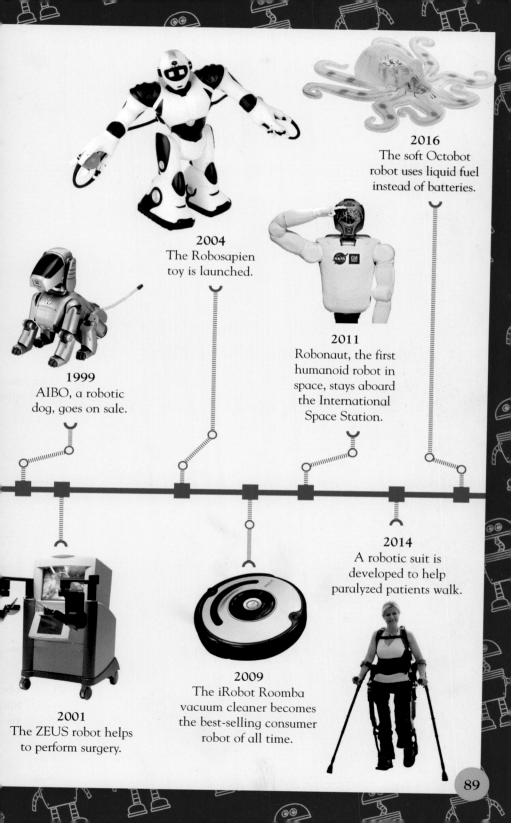

2016
The soft Octobot robot uses liquid fuel instead of batteries.

2004
The Robosapien toy is launched.

1999
AIBO, a robotic dog, goes on sale.

2011
Robonaut, the first humanoid robot in space, stays aboard the International Space Station.

2014
A robotic suit is developed to help paralyzed patients walk.

2001
The ZEUS robot helps to perform surgery.

2009
The iRobot Roomba vacuum cleaner becomes the best-selling consumer robot of all time.

Quiz

1. Which ancient Greek god made a giant bronze man called Talos?

2. Which burrowing animal has Daniel Goldman copied in his rescue robot design?

3. Who invented the first robot animal that could move around independently?

4. Where did the first RoboCup games take place?

5. Name the service robot that can iron clothes.

6. Which robot is also known as "The Cubinator"?

7. What are uncrewed robotic aircraft called?

8 Which robot unveiled in 2003 was designed to look like a young Japanese woman?

9 What was the name of the self-driving car project that Google started in 2009?

10 Who was the first person to operate a robotic limb with their brain?

Answers on page 93

Glossary

3-D printer
A machine that prints solid objects using layers of material, such as plastic.

aerial
Something moving or operating in the air.

animatronic
The use of machines or robots to make puppets and models move in a natural way. For example, the T. rex in *Jurassic Park* is an animatronic model.

artificial intelligence
The ability of a machine to think for itself.

automaton
A machine that works on its own without the need for human control.

autonomous
A machine that can carry out a job or function on its own.

biomimetic
A machine that mimics, or copies, the structures of living things.

circuit
A loop that an electric current travels around in.

data
A word for information.

humanoid
A machine with a similar appearance to a human.

Industrial Revolution
A period in history that started in the 18th century when machines first appeared in factories and were used to produce goods.

mechanism
A part of a machine that does a job to help make the machine work.

microphone
An electronic part through which sound is heard.

glider
An aircraft that has long wings and no engine, and flies by gliding.

programming
The task of creating instructions for a computer to follow, written in a special language.

rover
A vehicle that can drive over rough surfaces, for example the Mars Exploration Rover.

software
Programs on a computer that tell it how to work.

virtual
Something that exists digitally instead of in the real world.

Answers to the Quiz:

1. Hephaestus; **2.** The sandfish lizard; **3.** William Grey Walter; **4.** Japan; **5.** The Dressman; **6.** RuBot II; **7.** Drones; **8.** Actroid; **9.** Waymo; **10.** Jesse Sullivan

Guide for Parents

DK Readers is a four-level interactive reading adventure series for children, developing the habit of reading widely for both pleasure and information. These books have an exciting main narrative interspersed with a range of reading genres to suit your child's reading ability. Each book is designed to develop your child's reading skills, fluency, grammar awareness, and comprehension in order to build confidence and engagement when reading.

Ready for a *Reading Alone* book

YOUR CHILD SHOULD

- be able to read independently and silently for extended periods of time.
- read aloud flexibly and fluently, in expressive phrases with the listener in mind.
- be able to respond to what is being read and be able to discuss key ideas in the text.

A VALUABLE AND SHARED READING EXPERIENCE

Supporting children when they are reading proficiently can encourage them to value reading and to view reading as an interesting, purposeful, and enjoyable pastime. So here are a few tips on how to use this book with your child.

TIP 1 Reading aloud as a learning opportunity:

- after your child has read a part of the book, ask him/her to tell you what has happened so far.
- even though your child may be reading independently, most children at this level still enjoy having a parent read aloud. Take turns reading sections of the book, especially sections that contain dialogue that can provide practice in expressive reading.

TIP 2 Chat at the end of each chapter:

- encourage your child to recall specific details after each chapter.
- let your child pick out interesting words and discuss what they mean.
- talk about what each of you found most interesting or most important.
- ask the questions provided on some pages and in the quiz. These help to develop comprehension skills and awareness of the language used.
- ask if there's anything that your child would like to discover more about.

Further information can be researched in the index of other nonfiction books or on the Internet.

A FEW ADDITIONAL TIPS

- Continue to read to your child regularly to demonstrate fluency, phrasing and expression; to find out or check information; and for sharing enjoyment.
- Encourage your child to read a range of different genres, such as newspapers, poems, review articles, and instructions.
- Provide opportunities for your child to read to a variety of eager listeners, such as a sibling or a grandparent.

Series consultant, **Dr. Linda Gambrell**, Distinguished Professor of Education at Clemson University, has served as President of the National Reading Conference, the College Reading Association, and the International Reading Association.

Index